Ecosystems of North America

The Northern Forest

Greg Breining

BENCHMARK BOOKS

MARSHALL CAVENDISH
NEW YORK

Series Consultant: John T. Tanacredi, Ph.D., Supervisory Ecologist, National Park Service, U.S. Department of the Interior

Consultant: Richard Haley, Director, Goodwin Conservation Center

Benchmark Books
Marshall Cavendish Corporation
99 White Plains Road
Tarrytown, New York 10591-9001

Library of Congress Cataloging-in-Publication Data

Breining, Greg.
      The northern forest / Greg Breining.
          p.   cm. —(Ecosystems of North America)
      Includes bibliographical references and index.
      Summary: Explores the waters, trees, flowers, and animals of the northern forest, spreading from the
  St. Lawrence River and Great Lakes into Canada and Alaska, and their relationship to each other.
      ISBN 0-7614-0901-7 (lib. bdg.)
      1. Forest ecology—Canada—Juvenile literature. [1. Forest ecology. 2. Ecology.] I. Title. II. Series.
QH106.B74   2000   98-48644
577.3'0971—dc21   CIP
                                                                         AC

Photo Credits

The photographs in this book are used by permission and through the courtesy of:
Animals Animals/Earth Scenes: Michael F. Sacca 18; Johnny Johnson 20; Ken Cole 37; Francis Lepine 46. *Peter Arnold, Inc.:* Thomas D. Mangelsen front cover; Peter Arnold 54-55. *Photo Researchers, Inc.:* Pat and Tom Leeson 8; Rod Planck 17; S. Camazine/K. Visscher 24-25; Dr. Vic Bradbury (Science Photo Library) 28; Stephen J. Krasemann 34-35; Tracey Knauer back cover. *Tom Stack & Associates:* Thomas Kitchin 4-5, 11, 14-15, 31, 38, 39, 42-43, 48-49, 51, 56; Victoria Hurst 10; Erwin and Peggy Bauer 22; Diana L. Stratton 26; Spencer Swanger 30; John Shaw 32, 52; Rod Planck 40; John Gerlach 44; Dominique Braud 47, 58; Jeff Foott 50. Cover design by Ann Antoshak for BBI.

Series Created and Produced by BOOK BUILDERS INCORPORATED

Printed in Hong Kong
6 5 4 3 2 1

Contents

Exploring the Northern Forest

The northern forest spreads from the St. Lawrence River and the Great Lakes far into Canada and central Alaska. It is also called the boreal forest, northern coniferous forest, or simply the north woods. The northern forest seems somber, lonely, and ancient. A writer who sailed with a group of scientists along the north shore of Lake Superior in the mid-1800s wrote: "It was as if no noise had been heard here since the woods grew, and all Nature seemed sunk in a dead, dreamless sleep."

Let's imagine that you have hiked deep into this quiet forest. The trees you notice most are dark green evergreens, which keep their needlelike leaves all year long. These include spruce and firs, which are dense and triangular, like Christmas trees. The tallest evergreens are the white pine and the red pine. They may tower more than 100 feet (30 m) and grow too large to get your arms around.

But not all trees around you are evergreens. You will likely glimpse an aspen or a birch, whose leaves turn bright yellow in fall before they drop to the forest floor.

The tall trees form the **canopy**, the green cover of leaves and branches high overhead that, like an umbrella, blocks much of the sunlight.

Evergreens such as spruce, fir, and pine are plentiful in the northern forest.

Shrubs grow beneath the trees to form the **understory**. The kinds of plants that grow in the understory depend on the kind of soil and the amount of sunlight that penetrates the canopy. Low-growing plants, the **ground cover**, carpet the forest floor. Red bunchberries and bluebead lilies add splashes of color. In wet places, mosses grow soft and deep underfoot. On many cliffs and large boulders, you will find gray, green, and orange lichens, simple **organisms** that can survive on bare rock.

Nearly everywhere you go, you will discover clear lakes and streams. For thousands of years, humans have traveled the northern forests by canoe on a network of waterways. If you were to paddle through these same waters, you would hear the call of the white-throated sparrow and the racheting chatter of a red squirrel as it eats seeds from a pinecone. You might see a sharp-shinned hawk, one of many birds of prey that kill and eat small mammals and songbirds. You would probably spot a common loon, a large bird that dives for the fish living in the clear water. Perhaps you would see a moose swimming across a lake or eating aquatic plants along a muddy shore. On a quiet night at your campfire, you might hear the howls of a distant wolf pack.

A Sense of Place

Why do we find spruce trees, beavers, and wolves here in the northern forest, rather than magnolias, antelopes, and alligators? The answer can be found by studying the region's physical environment, especially its **climate**. (Climate is the pattern of weather in a region year-in and year-out.)

In the northern forest, summers are short and cool, and rainfall is moderate. Winters are long and bitterly cold, with temperatures occasionally dipping below minus 40 degrees Fahrenheit (minus 40° C). Snow covers the ground four to six months of the year; during winter, lakes are covered with ice. Plants and animals of the northern forest have developed ways to survive in these conditions, especially the long harsh winters, which animals and plants from warmer climates could not endure.

The Northern Forest

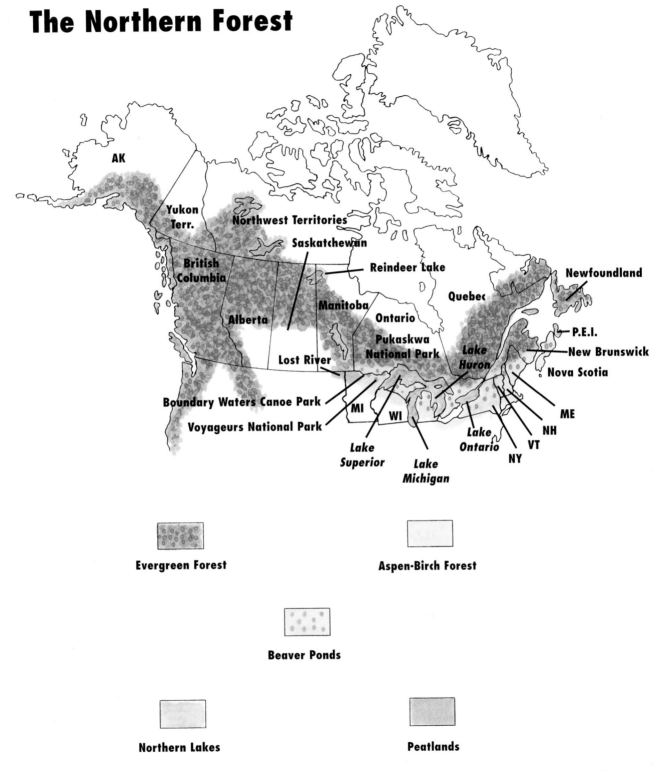

AK

Yukon
Terr.

Northwest Territories

Saskatchewan

British
Columbia

Reindeer Lake

Newfoundland

Quebec

Manitoba

Alberta

Ontario

P.E.I.

Pukaskwa
National Park

New Brunswick

Lost River

Lake
Huron

Nova Scotia

Boundary Waters Canoe Park

ME

Voyageurs National Park

MI

WI

Lake
Ontario

NH

VT

*Lake
Superior*

*Lake
Michigan*

NY

Evergreen Forest

Aspen-Birch Forest

Beaver Ponds

Northern Lakes

Peatlands

The northern forest stretches from the west coast of Alaska to Nova Scotia, on the eastern edge of Canada.

Bluebead lily and bunchberries grow on the forest floor, where a thick canopy of evergreens provides shade year-round.

Another key to understanding why certain plants and animals thrive in a region is found in its **soil**. The soil of the northern forest is thin and rocky in many places. Cliffs and bare rock line the shores of many lakes and rivers. Why is there so little soil here? For long stretches of time during the past several hundred thousand years, **continental glaciers**—vast sheets of ice hundreds of feet thick— covered the north country. In many places, the slowly moving glaciers scraped away the topsoil clear down to the bedrock. In the thousands of years since these glaciers disappeared, little additional soil has developed. The soil that is present has few nutrients because in this cold climate, the organisms that transform dead plants and animals into fertile soil work very slowly. The trees and plants that grow here must be able to survive in these poor, thin soils.

Making Connections

Each organism on Earth is surrounded by its **environment**—all the living and nonliving things that affect it, including the climate and soil. The study of the relationships between these living and nonliving things is called **ecology**.

The place where an animal lives is called its **habitat**. The habitat of the moose, for example, is the northern forest, where it can find aquatic plants and young trees for food and dense evergreens for shelter.

The moose, plants, and other animals that share an environment make up a **biological community**. One way to study this community is to look at the **food chain**, or who eats what. For example, the tender young shoots of the aspen are eaten by the moose, which is, in turn, eaten by wolves. *Aspen—moose—wolf* is one food chain in the northern forest.

Yet the word *chain* does not completely describe the complexity of relationships in the northern forest. For example, many animals besides moose—including ruffed grouse, beavers, white-tailed deer, and various insects—eat parts of the aspen tree. And wolves are not the only animals that eat moose. Infestations of ticks may kill adult moose in winter, and black bears may kill and eat moose calves in spring. Crows and carrion beetles may feed on the remains of a moose, even though they did not kill it. As you can see, the feeding relationships between organisms are too interwoven to be described as a simple chain. Together, they create what scientists call a **food web**.

Each organism in a biological community affects the plants and animals around it in indirect ways as well. The moose, for example, eats the branches of a young aspen tree, killing it or stunting its growth. The droppings that the moose leaves on the ground enrich the soil, helping other plants to grow. Wolves kill the moose for food. The leftovers may be eaten by foxes, ravens, and perhaps a wolverine. Thus, the aspen tree has an indirect relationship with the wolverine, even though the wolverine does not use the aspen for either food or shelter. All these relationships among the living and nonliving things in an environment form an **ecosystem**.

Common in the northern forest, moose browse on young deciduous trees, such as the aspen.

Energy Flow

Just as energy in the form of fuel runs an engine, energy in the form of stored chemicals runs through an ecosystem to sustain life. Energy enters the system as sunlight striking Earth. Green plants are able to capture the energy of sunlight through the process of **photosynthesis**. Using photosynthesis, they produce sugar molecules, the basis of new tissues. Plants are known as **producers** because they produce their own food. Plant-eaters, which may be as small as an insect or as large as a moose, are known as **primary consumers**. Predators, which eat other animals, are known as **secondary consumers**. The bacteria, fungi, and other small organisms that break down animal wastes and the remains of dead plants and animals are called **decomposers**.

Each of these links in a food chain is called a **trophic level**. When an organism at one trophic level is eaten by an organism at the next trophic level, about 90 percent of the energy in the eaten organism is lost. For example, when a snowshoe hare is eaten by a lynx, only about 10 percent of the energy in the hare is available to produce new tissue in the lynx. Most of the energy in the hare is lost as heat or eliminated by the lynx as waste.

Because of this loss of energy at each trophic level, the number of pro-

The wolf preys on much larger animals, including caribou, moose, and white-tailed deer.

ducers (plants) in an ecosystem is much greater than the number of primary consumers. And the number of primary consumers is much greater than the number of secondary consumers. There must be only a few large predators, such as wolves, lynxes, and wolverines, at the top of a food chain. Otherwise, they would run out of food and starve.

Nutrient Cycling

Nutrients, such as carbon and phosphorus, flow through the same food web in much the same way as energy, but with this difference: energy flow is a one-way trip. Energy is eventually lost and cannot be recovered by animals or plants. Our energy supply is, however, constantly replenished by the sun. Nutrients, on the other hand, are recycled over and over.

To better understand the **nutrient cycle**, let's imagine the path of a carbon atom. The atom is bonded with two oxygen atoms to form the colorless, odorless gas carbon dioxide. The carbon dioxide molecule is exhaled by a caribou and drifts in the air until it is trapped by a needle of a spruce tree. Through photosynthesis, the needle changes the carbon dioxide molecule into a complex molecule that is used to grow another needle on the tree. One winter day, the new needle is eaten by a spruce grouse. The grouse is soon eaten by a great gray owl. The carbon atom stays in the owl's body until the owl dies and decomposes on the forest floor. The carbon atom is then taken up by the roots of a cedar tree, where it forms part of the tree's inner wood. Decades later, the tree is consumed in a forest fire. The carbon atom is joined by two oxygen atoms and set free in the atmosphere as carbon dioxide once again.

Succession

The northern forest is always changing. It is abuzz with activity as plants and animals reproduce, grow, and die. Each organism affects those around it through the complicated relationships we have examined. Over time, these effects begin to add up and change the overall appearance and character of the forest. This process of change, much of which is predictable, is called **succession**.

The factors that drive succession are numerous and complex. Succession may begin with an event as simple as a lichen finding a foothold on bare rock and starting the long process of forming soil. At one time, scientists thought of succession as a gradual process that led to a predictable and final result called a **climax community.**

But ecologists have come to realize that succession is an ongoing process that is affected by disturbances, such as forest fires, powerful windstorms, diseases, and insect pests. These disturbances may happen frequently, or they may occur rarely. They may affect only a few acres or kill trees over many square miles. Because of these disturbances, a forest is actually made of small areas in various stages of succession.

In the following chapters, we will examine the plant and animal communities that make up the northern forest. We will also come to understand how succession changes the northern forest over time. As you will see, change is a continual and natural part of forest ecosystems.

Succession

Fire burns forest, which is replaced by...

Shrubs and trees grow, slowly changing the meadow into...

Beavers dam stream and eat aspen trees, forming...

Beavers move out, pond drains, and becomes a meadow...

This cycle of succession was greatly influenced by the beaver pond, but most succession is not.

A Harsh Life

Pukaskwa (pronounced PUK-a-saw) National Park sits on the Canadian shore of Lake Superior. In winter, winds whip across the rocky shores, and snow covers the land for several months. Temperatures plummet to far below zero, sometimes plunging below minus 40 degrees Fahrenheit (minus 40°C). Spring comes quickly, but summers are short and often cool. These harsh conditions rule the northern forest, forcing the plants and animals there to adapt or perish.

If you were to paddle a kayak along the coast of Pukaskwa National Park in spring, you would notice that many of the trees are still bare. The leaf buds are just beginning to turn light green. These are **deciduous** trees, which lose their leaves every fall and grow them again in the spring. The most common deciduous trees in the northern forest are aspen and birch.

Many other trees, you will notice, are dark green. These are evergreens, mainly white spruce, black spruce, and balsam fir. Instead of leaves, these trees have needles that contain **chlorophyll**. Like leaves, the needles capture the energy of sunlight through photosynthesis to produce sugars

In Pukaskwa National Park, stands of evergreens contrast with the light green of deciduous trees, such as birch and aspen.

that nourish the tree. Because the trees keep their needles all winter, photosynthesis takes place year-round. None of the trees' energy must be consumed in producing new needles. By keeping their needles, the trees also retain many minerals, so they can grow in the mineral-poor soil. The needles are covered by tough, thick tissue so they do not lose moisture during winter, when the air is cold and dry.

The seeds of spruce, fir, and other needle-bearing trees are contained in cones, so these trees are also called **conifers**. Where conifers are the dominant trees, the ground is covered with dead needles that make the soil acidic. Little light penetrates the dense canopy of needles to reach the forest floor. Many plants cannot survive in acidic soils and low light, so they do not grow in conifer **stands** (groups of trees of about the same age). Among the few trees that thrive in these conditions are beaked hazelnut, mountain maple, and feathermosses, which grow to luxurious thickness.

Forest Communities

In Pukaskwa, deciduous and coniferous trees form various communities, depending on conditions such as soils, moisture, and sunlight. Deciduous species, such as birch, aspen, and some red maple, grow quickly in clearings left by a windstorm or forest fire. As these trees grow, conifers such as balsam fir and white spruce sprout in the shady understory. Aspen and birch do not live long. As they age and die, the conifers take over the community.

Yet even as conifers dominate, the aspen and birch are waiting in the wings, prepared to take over again. Aspen are able to resprout from their underground roots, which live long after the tree above has died. Sprouts called "suckers" may appear up to 100

Before Pukaskwa became a park, loggers cut many of its spruce, fir, and jack pine. The logs were floated down rivers to Lake Superior, where mills ground them up to make paper. After logging, a new forest of deciduous trees began to grow. This change benefited the moose but made life more difficult for the caribou, which today are very scarce in the park. To save the caribou, we must preserve some of the old forest as it existed long ago.

feet (30 m) from the parent tree. Birches can resprout from the stumps of old trees. So after many decades, when the spruce and fir finally die from old age or disease and open the forest floor to sunlight once again, the aspen and birch are able to sprout quickly and get a head start on all the other trees.

Black spruce grow in areas that are too wet and dark for other plant species. Occasionally, spiders will spin their webs among the branches.

Old-man's beard, a lichen, grows on tree branches and serves as the main food of caribou.

Some plant communities win the battle of succession by grow-ing where few other plants will grow. The black spruce and feather-moss forest is a common example in Pukaskwa National Forest. Skinny black spruce grow close together. Because of the dense shade, few plants grow beneath the understory, except for a thick carpet of soft feathermosses. The black spruce and feathermoss are able to grow in low areas where soils are too wet for most other tree species. Even when spruce die of old age or are blown down by the wind, the only trees that can grow in their place are more black spruce. By growing in a habitat where most other plants cannot sur-vive, black spruce are present in every stage of succession.

Rock Gardens

Another organism that grows where few others can survive is lichen—a combination of a fungus and an alga that contains chlorophyll. The fungus clings to the rock, while the alga manufactures food for them both through photosynthesis. Alone, the fungus would starve, and the alga would be swept away by the first strong wind. With the two organisms working together, lichens can flourish on bare rock, even on the face of sheer cliffs. Lichens are often the first organisms to live in an area and are called a pioneer species.

Lichens perform an important role in the slow soil-building process. As they colonize on the bare rock, they trap bits of blowing sand, soil, leaves, and conifer needles. This absorbent material traps moisture. Other plants may then find a foothold on the rock. After these plants die, they decompose and contribute organic matter to the site, an essential step in forming fertile soil. After many centuries, a layer of soil begins to cover the rock. So, as lichens grow where few plants can, they gradually create conditions that allow other plants to grow and crowd them out.

An unusual plant called the Indian pipe has adapted to the difficult conditions underneath conifers. This plant has no chlorophyll for photosynthesis. Instead, its roots secrete a substance that attracts fungi. The fungi send out threads to penetrate the roots of the Indian pipe. The threads form a bridge that allows food to pass from the conifers through the fungi to the Indian pipe.

Living Together

One large mammal that has adapted to the climate and special plant communities of the northern forest is the woodland caribou. The caribou is a species of deer. It looks like the Old World reindeer, except that it is larger, weighing up to 600 pounds (273 kg). Well adapted to snow and cold, the caribou is covered with hollow hair shafts and thick underfur that trap air close to its body and keep it warm, even when it swims in icy water. The caribou's large feet help it walk on snow and boggy ground. Its main source of nourishment is lichens, and during the winter it paws through the snow with its hooves to reach them.

Moose are another large member of the deer family. They stand up to 6 feet (1.8 m) tall and weigh up to 1,200 pounds (564 kg). Their long legs enable them to run through deep snow to escape their chief predators, wolves. Unlike caribou, moose eat primarily the branches of small trees and shrubs, such as aspen, willow, and dogwood. Thus, moose are drawn to young forests that sprout in the wake of a windstorm or fire. Caribou, on the other hand, favor old forests with well-developed lichen communities.

The gray wolf is the most common large predator in the northern forest. Also called the timber wolf because of its habitat, it is closely related to the dog. Wolves live and hunt in family groups called packs. In the northern forest, their primary prey are moose, caribou, beavers, and snowshoe hares. Along the southern fringes of the northern forest, they eat white-tailed deer and occasionally livestock. They are very adaptable predators.

The complicated relationship between caribou, moose, and wolves demonstrates how succession can affect animals. For thousands of years, caribou and wolves lived together. Because wolves

Caribou, which thrive on lichen in old forests, have disappeared from large areas where loggers have cut the trees.

Know Your Conifers

Conifers, trees with seeds contained in cones, are hallmarks of the northern coniferous forest. All the conifers of the northern forest have needles or scaly leaves rather than the flat leaves. There are many kinds of conifers, but people often refer to all of them as "pine trees" or "Christmas trees." A good way to begin studying the northern coniferous forest is to learn to distinguish one conifer from another. Follow these steps (using a field guide will help).
You will need:
• leaves or needles from several conifers

1. If the leaves have scales that overlap like fish scales, go to step 2. If the leaves look like needles, go to step 3.

2. If some of the needles have sharp points and the cones look like dried-up berries, the tree is an **eastern red cedar**. If the needles are not sharp and the cones are woody, the tree is a **northern white cedar**.

3. If the needles are joined at the base in bundles of two to five needles, go to step 4. If the needles grow singly or in bunches of 12 or more, go to step 5.

4. If the needles are 2-1/2 to 5 inches (6–12 cm) long and grow in clusters of five, the tree is an **eastern white pine**. If the needles are 4 to 6 inches (10–15 cm) long and grow only two to a cluster, the tree is a **red pine** (also known as a Norway pine, even though it is native to North America). If the needles are only 3/4 to 1-1/2 inches (1.8–2.7 cm) long and grow two to a bunch, your tree is a **jack pine**.

5. If the needles are about 1 inch (2.5 cm) long, grow in clusters of 12 or more, and turn golden yellow in the fall, the tree is a **tamarack**. If the needles are flat, grow singly from each side of the branch, have a fleshy green point of attachment, and smell fresh and spicy when you crush them, the tree is a **balsam fir**. If the needles grow singly and are square in their cross-section (so you can roll them between your fingers), go to step 6.

6. If the needles are 1/3 to 3/4 inch (.8–1.8 cm) long and give off a strong odor when you crush them, the tree is a **white spruce**. If the needles are only 1/4 to 1/2 inch (.6–1.2 cm) long and have only a mild odor, it is a **black spruce**.

Padded feet allow the lynx to sneak up on snowshoe hares, which use their own large feet to race away from these predators.

find caribou calves easy prey, the caribou adapted in order to elude the wolves. Pregnant caribou would swim to desolate shorelines or islands, where wolves have difficulty following and finding them. The caribou would then give birth in safety. By winter, when wolves could walk over the ice to the refuges, the calves and cows had returned to the mainland. Without food, the wolves, too, would leave the calving areas.

But once the old forests were logged, moose ventured farther north to take advantage of the young trees that grew in the sunny openings of the newly cleared forests. Unlike the roaming caribou, moose occupy the same areas, including the caribou-calving grounds, year-round. Wolves no longer had to follow the elusive caribou but could stay in one place and prey on moose.

When the caribou returned to the calving grounds to give birth, the wolves were waiting for them. The wolves were able to kill caribou more easily than they could kill the larger, stronger moose. As a result, caribou quickly disappeared from most areas with high moose populations. In effect, the wolf, a predator of the moose, enabled the moose to succeed at the expense of the caribou.

While predators such as wolves will eat any animal small enough to kill, the Canada lynx depends almost entirely on the snowshoe hare. The hare is well adapted to the northern forest. It eats the plentiful bark, twigs, and leaves in the forest. The hare turns white in winter to blend in with the snow. Its large feet enable it to run across the snow, as if on snowshoes.

The lynx is a medium-sized wildcat that weighs up to 40 pounds (18 kg). Like the snowshoe hare, the lynx has large furry feet to run fast across the snow—so it can catch the hare.

The hare's population swings up and down for reasons that are not entirely clear. When there are plenty of hares, the lynx have food for their kittens and the lynx population grows. When hares are scarce, the lynx starve or produce few young. The well-being of the lynx depends entirely on the hare.

Two grouse of the northern forest demonstrate how similar species can occupy different habitats. Both of these birds look like small brown chickens. Each is a bit over a foot (30 cm) long. They take off quickly with an explosive flurry of wings. But their food habits send these two grouse to different parts of the forest. The ruffed grouse feeds heavily on fruits, berries, clover leaves, and the buds and flowers of aspen, alder, and birch. These foods abound in young deciduous forests. The spruce grouse, on the other hand, is able to digest the needles of conifers. So it spends much of its time in stands of conifers such as jack pine, black spruce, and tamarack, which are often found in older forests. When a conifer forest is destroyed by logging or fire and a deciduous forest grows in its place, spruce grouse disappear and ruffed grouse become common, simply because the available food has changed.

The plants and animals of the northern forest have adapted in many ways to the region's harsh climate. Their complex interactions allow them not only to survive, but to thrive.

Born of Fire

On a warm day in May, strong wind fanned the embers of a small fire in the woods of northern Minnesota. Flames began to spread through the dead leaves and needles on the forest floor. Soon fire shot into the trees and raced through the western portion of the Boundary Waters Canoe Area Wilderness. Needles of spruce, fir, and pine exploded into flame as the fire spread from treetop to treetop, racing high above the ground. The fire lasted for three days, until firefighters and spring rain and snow finally put it out. By then, more than 25 square miles (9.65 sq km) of timber had been destroyed.

This fire occurred in 1971. Named the Little Sioux Fire after a small river that runs through the area, it was one of the largest fires in the Boundary Waters in recent years. What happened afterward illustrates the importance of fire to the northern forest.

At first, the forest appeared to have been destroyed. For mile after mile, charred tree trunks lay on the burned ground or stood like ghostly sentinels. But with the canopy gone, sunlight flooded

As forest fires destroy some forest communities, they give a head start to new ones, such as stands of birch and aspen.

*Soon after fire burns away the dense
canopy of evergreens, aspen and
birch sprout in the sunny openings.*

the bare ground, warming the blackened remains.
Within weeks, new growth had appeared—first
spotted grasses, sedges, and bluebead lilies and then
bracken ferns and sprouts of aspen, red maple, and
willow. Jack pine seedlings took root—as many
as 20,000 in an area the size of a football field.

Soon the new growth attracted moose.
They ate aspen, willows, and fire cherry. Deer
appeared in low, moist areas to feed on fireweed,
jewelweed, and mountain maple. Bark beetles
and other insects infested the dead but still-standing
trees. Woodpeckers of several species became
more abundant than ever before.

As you can see, many species of plants and
animals respond favorably to forest fire. The northern
forest, especially along the warmer, drier southern
and western fringes, is a fire-dependent ecosystem.
Foresters divide these forest fires into three types.
One type is ground fires, which burn the top layer
of the soil but do not reach far above the surface.
The second type is surface fires, which burn forest
undergrowth and the litter on the forest floor. The
third type, crown fires, helped spread the flames at
the Boundary Waters Canoe Area Wilderness. Crown
fires advance through the tops of trees or shrubs.
Two or even all three types of fires can occur in the
same area at the same time.

Evolution of the Forest

To better understand the history of fire in the forest, scientists devised a way to look back more than 10,000 years. They drove pipes into the bottom of small lakes to collect **core samples**. They removed these samples from the pipes and studied the layers of muck that had been deposited year after year on the lake bottom. Each layer contained pollen from the trees and other plants growing in the forest at the time. Each kind of pollen could be identified under a microscope.

Scientists could determine, for example, that immediately after the glaciers receded, about 10,000 years ago, the area was covered with tundra and scattered spruce trees—much like the arctic regions of today. But as the climate continued to warm, pine trees appeared. The climate apparently became much warmer than it is now because eastern hardwoods such as walnut and hickory sprang up. These trees could not withstand the cold temperatures in the north woods today.

Eventually the climate cooled again, the warm-climate trees disappeared, and the forest we see today gradually developed. During all this time, charcoal from forest fires collected at the bottom of the lakes. The charcoal in the core samples indicated that fire had always been a part of these forests.

An **ecologist** named Miron Heinselman traveled throughout the Boundary Waters estimating the age of trees and looking for **fire scars**—injuries to trees from past fires. He was able to determine that nearly every part of the Boundary Waters had burned at one time or another. During drought, large areas would burn in a single season. Virtually all the stands of trees in the forest had grown on land that had been badly burned by a fire. Like an artist working on a large canvas, fire had painted the broad patterns of the forest.

How do all these fires start? Many are sparked by lightning. During the middle of summer, so-called dry lightning storms sweep through areas such as the Boundary Waters. During these storms, rain does not fall, or it evaporates before hitting the ground. The lightning often strikes rocky areas covered by a thin layer of lichen or dried-out needles, which burst into flame.

*With many of
the fires that
are touched
off in the
north woods,
lightning is
the culprit.*

Humans, who have lived in the northern forest for thousands of years, are the other cause of fire. Indians would often set fire to the forest to clear out underbrush to improve the habitat for animals such as moose and to encourage the growth of sun-loving plants such as blueberries. Today, wilderness campers and landowners who live near the Boundary Waters set fires accidentally.

Helping Plants to Grow

Before a fire, many of the ecosystem's nutrients are stored in dead needles, leaves, twigs, bark, and wood. As an intense fire burns these materials, great amounts of phosphorus, potassium, magnesium, calcium, and iron are released as ash and become mixed into the soil. Burning away the dead leaves and needles that cover the forest floor also provides a good seedbed for new plants. Following the fire, sunlight bathes the open ground, encouraging the growth of small plants that cannot survive in the deep shade of a mature forest.

Certain plant communities are able to take advantage of the conditions created by a fire. Aspen and birch, for example, sprout more quickly than other species and soon fill the space left by a major fire. Both species produce large numbers of seeds that are blown great distances by the wind, reseeding areas scorched by fire.

The seeds of jack pine grow in cones sealed tight with resin produced by the tree. Forest fires usually kill mature jack pines, but the heat loosens the resin. Soon after the fire, the cones spring open and drop the seeds on the bare ground, where they take root even when the ashes are still warm. Black spruce also have cones that drop seeds after a fire. Both jack pine and black spruce are able to colonize an area cleared by fire and dominate the stand for many years.

Every year, lightning sparks 75,000 forest fires in the United States. Along with starting fires to promote succession and species diversity, lightning releases nitrogen into the atmosphere. The nitrogen is carried to the ground in raindrops and enriches the soil, further helping the forest to grow.

Sprouting from stumps, birch saplings can quickly dominate a new forest.

    The forest fires that visited areas such as the Boundary Waters left behind vast stands of tall red pine and white pine. These pines prosper in the special conditions created by forest fire. Both species need clear ground and lots of sunlight to take root and grow as seedlings. For the first fifty years, they are vulnerable to new fires. After that, their large size and thick bark protect them from small fires. Their branches are clustered around the upper half of the tree, so small fires cannot climb into the crown and kill the trees.

During the 1800s and early 1900s, loggers cut these valuable pines, beginning in the northeastern United States and moving through the Great Lakes region. Sawmills cut the trees into lumber that helped build cities in the Northeast, the Midwest, and southern Canada.

Unfortunately, the loggers cut nearly all the mature pine trees and made little effort to replant trees. As a result, very few large stands of red pine and white pine exist in the forest today. Only in

Red pine and white pine saplings require lots of sunlight and open area to grow.

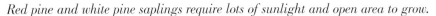

After surviving a fire deep in their burrows, deer mice emerge to feast on the seeds of jack pine and black spruce.

protected areas do pine trees grow tall and in great numbers as they once did. Because these tall pines are both beautiful and valuable, foresters have begun putting great effort into planting and growing pine forests. In some cases, foresters set fires on purpose to clear out underbrush and help the pine trees to grow.

Surviving Fire

Most forest fires are not as harmful to animals as you might believe. Most birds fly out of harm's way. Many large animals outrun the flames. Small mammals such as voles, mice, and chipmunks survive all but the hottest fires in underground burrows and then quickly repopulate a burn. Surveys made three weeks after the Little Sioux

Fire found little difference in the number of these small animals at the burn site and in the nearby forest.

We have already seen how deer and moose visit a burn to feed on new shoots of aspen and other plants. Many other animals benefit from forest fires as well. Populations of seed eaters such as deer mice explode as they feed on the newly released seeds of jack pine and black spruce. Black bears find raspberries and blueberries growing in the sunny openings left by fire. After several years, when ground cover has grown back to its original thickness and saplings are several feet high, animals such as ruffed grouse and snowshoe hares find the habitat ideal.

Other animals disappear until the forest gets older. Squirrels, for example, must live elsewhere until a mature canopy develops. Birds such as the black-throated warbler and pine warbler, which live in mature forests, also disappear until the forest ages.

During the past several decades, people have been successful in fighting forest fires in areas such as the Boundary Waters. Campers have taken Smokey Bear's warnings to heart and have been careful to prevent forest fires. Fires that do start are put out more quickly. This might seem like progress, but some plant communities, such as the stands of white pine and red pine, may gradually disappear from areas where fires are not allowed to burn. Ecologists have suggested various ways to reintroduce fire to the northern forest, such as letting natural fires burn and intentionally setting fires when the conditions are right.

Catastrophic disturbances such as forest fire have played a tremendous role in guiding and driving the succession of plant and animal communities in the northern forest. Despite the apparent destruction, forest fires are natural and largely beneficial. Without fire, the northern forest as we know it would be a very different place.

Cold, Clear Waters

*W*hen the continental glaciers retreated from the area that is now the northern United States and Canada, they left behind a bleak, gray land of bare rock and uneven deposits of sand and gravel. Depressions in the landscape filled with water, forming hundreds of thousands of lakes. Some were no more than small ponds; others covered thousands of square miles. One of these large lakes is Reindeer Lake in northern Saskatchewan and Manitoba, named after the woodland caribou that live nearby.

Swept by wind, Reindeer Lake is surrounded by a forest of dark, scrubby jack pine and spruce. More than 100 miles (161 km) long, the lake is dotted with islands. Its shores are rocky. Like many lakes of the northern forest, it is clear and very deep—more than 600 feet (183 m) deep in places. It usually freezes over by early December and remains coated by ice until late May.

Watery Food Webs

Lakes have food chains and food webs, just as land environments do. The richness and abundance of

The waters of Reindeer Lake are clear and cold, and the lake bottom is rocky. With few nutrients available, water plants are sparse.

these food webs depends largely on the fertility of the water. The clear, cold lakes of the northern forest, like the land that surrounds them, are not fertile because the glacial rock and sand that form the lake bed have few nutrients to dissolve in the water. These infertile lakes are called **oligotrophic**. (More fertile lakes are called **mesotrophic**; very fertile lakes are **eutrophic**.)

Because of the low fertility, few plants grow in these rock-lined basins. With few plants at the base of the food chain, there are few primary consumers, and thus even fewer secondary consumers. A eutrophic lake in the eastern forest region or prairies of the United States can easily produce ten times as many pounds of fish per acre as oligotrophic lakes such as Reindeer.

While the lack of nutrients limits the abundance of the aquatic community, the cold conditions and young age of the lakes in the northern forest limit its complexity as well. Lakes in the northern forest were formed after the glaciers receded. Only a few fish species could survive the cold conditions at the margins of the glaciers and establish themselves in these lakes. In the relatively short time since, the lakes' plant and animal communities have not evolved a great deal and so are not very complicated or diverse.

A few plants grow along the shore and in the shallows of Reindeer Lake, but most of the food production begins with free-floating microscopic organisms called **plankton**. Some of these are tiny plants called **phytoplankton**. Other plankton consists of small animals called **zooplankton**. Insects, crustaceans, and small fish eat these plankton.

In Reindeer and most other large lakes of the northern forest, the plankton, insects, and small fish are eaten by suckers, lake whitefish, and lake herring. These fish are eaten, in turn, by walleyes, northern pike, and lake trout. Because the water is cold and ice covered much of the year, fish grow slowly. But given enough time, they become quite large. Walleyes, valued by anglers for their delicate taste, grow up to 10 pounds (4.5 kg).

The lakes and rivers provided a highway for Indians to travel throughout the northern forest. The Cree Indians, who still live in the region, were skilled builders and paddlers of bark canoes. Other tribes of the northern forest, such as the Dene and Ojibwe, also depended on fish of the northern lakes for food.

Northern pike, hard-fighting fish with mouths full of long, sharp teeth, reach 30 pounds (13.6 kg), while lake trout, which live in deep open water, can weigh more than 50 pounds (22.7 kg).

Large fish are not the only predators to occupy the top of the Reindeer Lake food chain. River otters have long streamlined bodies, webbed feet, and broad tails that allow them to swim fast underwater and snap up fish. Long whiskers help them to locate food in dark or muddy water. Curious and playful, otters often circle boats or canoes. Besides fish, they eat frogs, clams, snails, and crayfish.

Fish grow slowly in this cold, clear lake, which was carved out by glaciers long ago.

Strong swimmers, river otters feed on fish, crayfish, and other small aquatic animals in the clear lakes and streams of the northern forest.

Several birds also perch atop the aquatic food chain. The common loon is a symbol of wilderness. It is a streamlined bird with webbed feet set toward the rear of its body. It can barely walk on land but swims fast in pursuit of fish, crayfish, and other aquatic organisms. The loon produces several strange calls, including a long mournful wail and a unique yodel.

The osprey, also known as a fish hawk, soars above the water. If it spots a fish near the surface, it dives and snatches it in its talons. The bald eagle fishes the same way; it will also steal a fish from an osprey in midair.

The white pelican traps small fish in shallow water and gobbles them up with its huge, pouched bill. With an 8-foot (2.4-m) wingspan, it is one of the largest birds in North America.

Staying Put

Aquatic plant and animal communities are determined by their physical environment, just as land-based communities are. But aquatic communities are much less prone to change and succession than forest communities. The reason? In part, the communities are simpler, with fewer competitors to take over. But the main reason is that there are few catastrophic disturbances in the aquatic ecosystem. No events equivalent to a forest fire get rid of the old communities, release nutrients, and unleash the forces of succession. Over thousands of years, aquatic communities in the northern forest have reached a climax state.

The eerie cries of the loon echo across the lakes of the northern forest. The loon can swim fast underwater to catch fish.

The rocky streams of the northern forest are vulnerable to pollution from human activities.

Where there have been changes, it is usually because of human activities. In Lake Superior, for example, loggers choked the streams flowing into the lake with logs, and sawmills polluted the bays with sawdust and wood waste destroying spawning areas for species such as lake sturgeon.

In the lakes, commercial fishers netted most of the large lake trout. The construction of a canal allowed sea lampreys to enter the Great Lakes from the Atlantic Ocean and kill many of the remaining lake trout. Sea lampreys are parasites that attach themselves to the trout with a sucking disk and feed on the fish's blood. Government programs in Canada and the United States have been helping since the 1970s to reduce the number of lampreys. Ships entering the harbors of Lake Superior have brought creatures from foreign lands, such as a perchlike predator called the ruffe and zebra mussels. Zebra mussels compete with native species for the algae in the lakes and absorb toxic substances from the water. When the mussels are eaten by fish or birds, these poisons move up the food chain.

Pesticides from farms and other pollutants from industries have contaminated Lake Superior and the other Great Lakes, causing birds such as the bald eagle to lay thin-shelled eggs that break before they hatch. These changes have had an upsetting effect on the plant and animal communities. Some species, such as lake trout and bald eagles, became very scarce and have recovered only as environmental threats have been reduced. Some contamination remains in the lakes, however. In many areas, people have been asked to eat fewer fish from the lakes because of the level of toxic substances they carry.

Most lakes of the northern forest, such as Reindeer Lake, have fared much better. Except for some fishing, humans have had little effect on the aquatic environment. As a result, the plant and fish communities remain much as they have for centuries.

Many lakes in the northern forest have been polluted by mercury. This heavy metal has been transported through the atmosphere from industries hundreds of miles away. Animals at the top of the food chain, such as lake trout and loons, collect high concentrations of the poisonous metal. The mercury can make lake trout unsafe to eat and kill birds or cause them to have difficulty reproducing.

Land That Shakes

At a place called Lost River in northern Minnesota, the ground quakes as you walk on it, almost as if it were pudding. The land is covered by a stubble of black spruce and tamarack trees. They are runty and scraggly, even though some of them are quite old.

Lost River is a **peatland**, a waterlogged landscape covered with peat, a mucky and spongy mass of largely undecayed organic material. Lost River resembles other peatlands that cover millions of acres throughout the northern forest. They are called a variety of names, including bogs, fens, moors, and mires.

Disappearing Lakes

Peatlands provide another example of how the northern forest has changed through succession. When the glaciers retreated, grasslike plants called sedges grew around the edges of the thousands of ponds and small lakes left behind. As these plants died, they fell into the water. Because the ponds were formed on bare rock or nutrient-poor sand, many were slightly acidic. They were also cold and stagnant.

In flat, waterlogged areas, dead plants accumulate in a spongy mass called peat.

Under these harsh conditions, the bacteria, worms, and other decomposers in the ponds could not work very fast or live in great numbers. As a result, the dead plant material never decayed. Instead it built up in deep layers of peat around the edges of the pond, eventually filling in the open water. Over time, shrubs and trees began to grow on this accumulating peat, which has completely filled some ponds and small lakes.

The peatland at Lost River, like many large peatlands in the north, formed in a different way. It was created by a process called **swamping**. Lost River lies on the very flat land that once formed the bottom of a huge glacial lake. When the lake drained away at the end of the Ice Age, the land remained water soaked. Few decomposers could live in the cold, continually wet conditions. Sedges and other plants died, forming a sodden mat. As plants grew on this soggy mass and then died themselves, the layer grew. It held water like a giant sponge. It also dammed natural drainage, forming shallow ponds. These, too, eventually filled with dead vegetation. Over time, this undecomposed vegetation accumulated and deepened to many feet deep, spreading for many miles across the land. Nutrients such as

The carnivorous pitcher plant traps and digests insects in its fluid-filled "pitcher."

carbon, hydrogen, oxygen, and nitrogen, which normally would have cycled through the ecosystem as organisms decomposed, were locked in the peat.

If you were to fly over Lost River, you would see subtle features created by the slow movement of water and the accumulation of dead plants. Many of these features look like ocean waves. Slightly raised islands of tamarack and black spruce look like battleships at sea. These **patterned peatlands** sweep across thousands of square miles of Alaska and Canada.

Peatland Plants and Animals

Many plants will not grow in peatlands, but some do thrive here. Grasslike sedges are common. So is a thick green moss called sphagnum. In fact, sphagnum ensures its survival by making its immediate surroundings more hostile to other plants and more favorable to itself. It soaks up water, so the area remains too waterlogged for many other plants (except peatland species) to survive. The sphagnum also absorbs certain nutrients that other plants need. The remaining substances in the water combine with hydrogen to form acids, which sphagnum can withstand but most other plants cannot. If you are a plant, sphagnum makes an unpleasant neighbor.

The pitcher plant has adapted in an unusual way to this nutrient-poor environment. Unable to draw much sustenance from the soil, it captures and digests insects instead. Its long, deep, trumpet-shaped leaf collects rainwater and other liquids at its base. The smell of the solution invites insects to crawl inside, but downward-pointing hairs inside the plant prevent them from crawling back out. When the insects tumble into the liquid, they are digested by its enzymes and bacteria, and the nutrients in their bodies are absorbed by the plant. Interestingly, certain species of mosquitoes, flies, moths, and aphids have adapted to these

In the peatlands of northern Europe, people have discovered hundreds of "bog bodies." They are the corpses of Iron Age men and women, preserved by the lack of oxygen and acidic water. They were buried in the peat up to 2,000 years ago.

conditions and are able to live in pitcher plants without getting trapped or digested.

Other peatland plants have different adaptations to help them survive the wet, oxygen-poor conditions in which they live. Black spruce, cedar, and tamarack avoid drowning in the waterlogged peat by sending out new roots from their trunks into the upper layers of peat, which hold the most oxygen. As the peat grows deeper, trees send out new roots. Members of the heath family have thick, leathery leaves to prevent loss of water during cold winters, when water at the roots may be frozen and unavailable to the plant.

Wildlife is usually scarce in the harsh environment of the bog. Ruffed, spruce, and sharp-tailed grouse all live in peatland. Gray wolves and moose may pass by. Farther north in Canada, woodland caribou eat the old-man's beard lichen that grows among the branches of the black spruce in peatlands. Chubby bog lemmings dote on grasses and sedges and nest in clumps of sphagnum. The water shrew has stiff hairs on its hind feet to aid in swimming. It feeds on slugs, earthworms, and spiders. Some threatened and rare birds—such as the sharp-tailed sparrow, sora rail, great gray owl, and short-eared owl—live in peatlands. While all of these animals are found there, none live exclusively in peatlands.

When startled, the spruce grouse bursts into flight with a flurry of wings and a loud, whirring sound.

Great gray owls are among the winged predators in the northern forests.

Succession

What becomes of a peatland over time? Does it turn into a different kind of plant and animal community through the process of succession? Or is it a climax community—where succession has hit a dead end? Scientists are not sure of the answer, but many believe that the conditions in a peatland generally become wetter, more acidic, and less hospitable to all but a few plant species. Apparently, once a peatland, always a peatland. If, however, the climate were to become warmer through either natural or human-caused global warming, the peat would dry out. Then the decomposers could go to work, breaking down the peat into soil. A different kind of forest could take root, and the land might no longer shake.

Nature's Engineers

*P*erhaps no animal in the northern forest has such an obvious effect on its habitat as the beaver. Beavers cut trees, build houses and dams, dig tunnels, and flood large areas of forest. Only humans can claim to rearrange the environment more than the beaver does. The beaver performs these chores to ensure its own survival. In the process, it has a tremendous effect on the plants and animals in its immediate environment and alters the course of succession.

Beavers are well adapted to live in water. They have flat tails and webbed feet for swimming, valves in their noses and ears to shut out water, and transparent membranes to shield their eyes as goggles would. Their lips close behind their teeth so they can carry branches without drowning. Their large, fast-growing front teeth are designed for gnawing.

Beavers dig burrows in riverbanks or build dome-shaped lodges of sticks and mud. In either style of dwelling, they enter through underwater tunnels and climb upward to a living chamber that is snug and dry above the waterline.

A beaver dam can flood a wide area, dramatically affecting the ecosystem there.

Beavers, which may weigh more than 60 pounds (27 kg), eat aquatic plants and the bark of aspen, willow, and alder. They waddle ashore to down trees with their sharp teeth, cutting off the smaller branches and carrying them back to their den so they can eat the bark. They anchor some branches underwater with mud and rocks to provide food during the winter.

To evade predators such as the wolf, the beaver family must have water deep enough to cover their entrance tunnels and their winter food stores. Water must also reach food supplies. To provide water of adequate depth, beavers often build dams of mud and sticks on small forest streams to create ponds or small lakes. The flooding that results may affect large areas. In Voyageurs National Park in northern Minnesota, for example, beavers have built dams on nearly all the small streams in the park. Their ponds cover more than 10 percent of the park's area.

The creation of a pond has a profound effect on the environment and guides the course of succession. As water rises, it drowns and kills trees. After a few years, dead, gray trees stand in the pond

After beavers ate or carried away this aspen's branches, twigs, and bark, all that remains is a stump.

Woodpeckers search tree bark for insects and drill cavities in trunks for nesting.

and ring its shore. This deadwood provides food and homes for many kinds of insects. Woodpeckers and other birds visit to eat the insects. Aquatic plants such as lily pads, irises, and arrowhead grow around the pond.

By flooding new areas of the forest, beavers gain access to new supplies of food. They eat the aspen seedlings that compete with pine seedlings. Thus, beavers may help a pine forest grow in areas where otherwise mainly aspen would live.

The pond benefits not only the beaver, but also other water-loving animals, including ducks, muskrats, and mink. Great blue herons may wade the edges of the pond, snatching fish and frogs with their long bills. Beaver ponds can also affect fish life. Trout live

Water lilies grow in shallow ponds, protected bays, and slow-moving streams.

in many small northern streams. As the trout grow larger, they run out of room to hide in these tiny streams and become exposed to predators such as herons or otters. A beaver pond provides a refuge of deep water, helping larger trout survive.

But beaver dams and ponds can also harm trout. The water in a broad, shallow pond is quickly warmed by the sun. The water may become too warm for trout to survive. Whether a pond benefits trout or harms them depends on the water temperature. If there are plenty of springs to cool the pond, the effect will be beneficial.

As beavers inhabit a pond or lake for many years, they cut down and eat the best food trees from the shoreline. When they can no longer find food around their pond, they may leave. Or they may be killed by wolves as they wander far into the woods to look for food. Without constant maintenance, the dams the beavers build will leak and fall apart, and the level of the pond will drop. The soils will dry out. The aquatic plants will die, and trees such as birch and aspen will take root.

On the other hand, when food becomes scarce, the beavers may build their dam even higher or build a new dam and flood more land, extending their influence over an ever-greater portion of the forest. Wherever beavers live, they strongly influence the environment, both directly and indirectly.

Beavers played an important role in the European exploration of the northern forests during the 1700s and 1800s. To get beaver fur for fashionable hats, French and British companies established posts throughout the northern forest. At the posts, French-Canadian canoeists called "voyageurs" traded knives, hatchets, and kettles to Indians for the fur of beavers the Indians had trapped. The fur companies created many of

Tomorrow's Forest

*M*uch of the northern forest is too far away, too remote, and too sparsely populated to have been changed much by humans. Vast regions remain undisturbed, appearing as they have for hundreds of years. Caribou, moose, black bears, wolves, lynx, and other large animals continue to exist in relatively high numbers. These regions can still properly be called wilderness.

But in large regions, modern society is having a profound effect on the appearance and functioning of the northern forest. Human activities are interfering with the ecological relationships and altering the succession of the forest. Some of these changes are clearly harmful; others are simply changes. Whether we allow them depends on what we as a society wish the northern forest to look like in the years ahead.

Trends and Challenges

As we have seen, forest fire has long played an important role in shaping the northern forest. Some plant communities, such as pine forests, would barely survive without frequent forest fires. When areas such as the Boundary Waters Canoe Area were first set aside to protect the wilderness character of the land, managers tried to prevent forest

Every year, thousands of canoeists and anglers enjoy the Boundary Waters Canoe Area, which was once logged for its pine, spruce, and fir.

Logging requires the use of large, heavy machinery.

fire. As a result, pine forests have gradually become overgrown with species such as spruce and fir. To restore the original plant communities, managers in some parks and other protected areas have begun to set some fires intentionally or to let some wildfires burn.

Logging continues to have a profound and widespread effect on the northern forest. Companies still cut pine for lumber and aspen, jack pine, spruce, and fir for pulpwood to make paper. Much of this wood is harvested in clear-cuts, meaning that loggers cut all the standing trees of suitable size over dozens or hundreds of acres. The result is a large opening much like that left by a forest fire. Moose and white-tailed deer find plenty to eat when young trees, such as aspen, sprout and grow in the sunny opening. But caribou and many songbirds disappear from regions where clear-cuts have broken up the forest.

The manufacture of paper from pulpwood is one of the major industries of the northern forest. Pulp mills break wood into fibers that can be used to make paper. These mills have polluted the air and water. Fish caught downstream from pulp mills often contain higher-than-normal amounts of mercury, a poisonous heavy metal. The mercury can make the trout unsafe to eat in great numbers. Pulp mills also pollute water with a family of toxic chemicals called dioxins, some of which may cause cancer. In some streams, such as the Rainy River along the northern Minnesota border, pulp-mill pollution has rendered fish unsafe to eat in great numbers.

Emissions from power plants and other industries in big cities of the eastern and midwestern United States have polluted clear lakes and streams in the northern forest. The forest is far removed from the nearest industry, but pollutants emitted into the atmosphere can be carried aloft for hundreds of miles before falling back to Earth.

During the last decade, scientists have debated whether pollution from burning fossil fuels will cause world climate to change and temperatures to rise. If this global warming does occur, forests around the world, including the northern forest, will probably change drastically.

The northern forest experienced widespread climate change once before, when the temperature gradually warmed after the Ice Age and then cooled to become the climate we have today. These changes suggest what might happen if the world's temperatures rise again. As before, the prairies and hardwood forests would probably push farther north. The northern forest would likely retreat to the north. If the warmer climate creates drier conditions, forest fires may become more frequent. Fire-dependent species such as white pine, red pine, and jack pine might become more common, depending on human management of these species. Animals along the southern fringe of the northern forest, such as white-tailed deer, would probably move northward. Creatures of the far north, such as caribou, might retreat even farther to the north.

In the fall, the brilliant colors of the maples and other deciduous trees attract many tourists.

Looking to the Future Forest

What will be the future of the northern forest? That is up to our decisions as a society. Logging undoubtedly will continue to be a major industry in the northern forest region. But if mature forest communities are to continue to flourish, some areas must remain closed to large-scale clear-cuts. Environmental groups and governments will have to continue to insist that industries such as power plants and the pulp mills clean up their air and water pollution.

Scientists and professional land managers will continue to work to better understand the individual plants and animals that live in the northern forest. More important, they will try to learn more about the relationships between these organisms and the forces of succession—the way in which the forest changes over time. By beginning to explore and understand the northern forest, you have taken a first step toward ensuring its future.

Collecting Leaves and Plants

A fun way to learn to identify trees, shrubs, and other plants is to collect leaves, flowers, or whole plants. You can preserve them with a simple leaf press.
You will need:

- two boards the same size, such as 8 by 10 inches (20 by 25 cm)
- several pieces of thick corrugated cardboard cut to the same dimensions as the boards
- a supply of newspaper or paper towels
- several strong rubber bands

1. Collect fresh leaves or flowers that are in good condition. If you see a small plant that you know to be common, clip it at the base. Collect the whole plant only if you see many others like it. Take notes about where you found the plant. Was the soil rocky, sandy, or loamy? Was the site wet? What kinds of other plants are nearby?

2. Place each specimen between sheets of paper. Then sandwich the paper and specimen between sheets of cardboard. The tunnels in the cardboard allow air to circulate and dry the specimens. Press several cardboard-paper-specimen sandwiches between the boards and secure the bundle with rubber bands.

3. Let the specimens dry for two to three days.

4. When your specimen is dry, display it by gluing it to paper or boxboard.

5. Use a field guide to identify the plant. Write its common name and scientific name on your display. Include other information, such as the date when you gathered the specimen and characteristics of the site where it grew.

Glossary

biological community   all of the plants and animals that share a particular environment.

canopy   the top layer of the forest, formed by the branches and leaves of the tallest trees, which blocks much of the sunlight.

chlorophyll   the green pigment found in plant cells.

climate   the pattern of weather in a region year-round.

climax   a community at the final stage of succession. It is capable of indefinite self-perpetuation under stable climatic and environmental conditions.

conifers   trees whose seeds are enclosed in a cone. Conifers—spruce, fir, pine, and cedar—have needles.

continental glaciers   vast sheets of ice hundreds of feet thick.

core sample   a portion of soil or even rock taken by driving a pipe or special drill into the ground. A core sample allows geologists to study layers of soil or bedrock, including those on the bottoms of lakes.

deciduous   trees whose leaves fall off every autumn and sprout again in spring.

decomposer   an organism that obtains its energy by breaking down animal wastes and dead organisms.

disturbances   events such as forest fires, windstorms, disease, and insect pests that remove or kill plants and alter the course of succession.

ecologist   a scientist who studies the relationships among species and their environment.

ecology   the study of the relationships among species and their environment.

ecosystem   the association and interactions of organisms and the physical environment.

environment   all the living organisms and nonliving things that somehow affect it, such as water and nutrients in the soil.

eutrophic   very fertile; a term used to describe lakes that are rich in nutrients and very productive of plant and animal life.

fire scars   injuries to trees caused by forest fires.

food chain   the progression of feeding relationships, beginning with plants and ending with a predator that is rarely killed and eaten by other animals. One food chain in the northern forest begins with plants such as the aspen tree, continues with the moose, and ends with the wolf, which is said to occupy the top of the food chain.

food web   the sum of many food chains, representing the many complicated food relationships between plants and animals.

ground cover   low plants that carpet the forest floor.

habitat   the place with the necessary food, shelter, and other living and nonliving things an animal needs to live.

mesotrophic   having moderate fertility; used to describe a lake.

nutrient cycle   the process by which nutrients, such as carbon, phosphorus, and calcium, flow through the food web, passing from one organism to another and eventually being released for reuse. Nutrients are recycled over and over.

oligotrophic   a term describing infertile lakes of low productivity.

organism   a living thing, such as a plant or animal.

patterned peatlands   vast areas of peat characterized by subtle patterns determined by the flow of water through the peat. Patterned peatlands cover thousands of square miles of northern Minnesota, Canada, and Alaska.

peatland   a wetland with conditions that prevent or slow the process of decomposition. The accumulation of sodden undecayed plant material is known as peat.

photosynthesis   the process by which plants and other organisms that have chlorophyll use light, carbon dioxide, and water to make sugar molecules and other substances.

phytoplankton   microscopic aquatic algae that contain chlorophyll and are capable of photosynthesis.

plankton   microscopic organisms that drift in lakes, rivers, or oceans. They form the basis of most aquatic food chains.

primary consumer   an animal that eats plants.

producer   an organism, usually a plant, that converts solar energy to chemical energy by photosynthesis.

secondary consumer   an animal that feeds on another animal.

soil   a mixture of minerals, other rock particles, and decayed matter.

stand   a distinct group of trees, usually dominated by trees of about the same age. In the northern forest, most stands get their start in a disturbance, such as a windstorm or fire, that removes the previous trees growing in the area.

succession   the process by which a biological community changes over a long time. Succession is largely determined by the physical environmental and influenced by various disturbances.

swamping   the process by which vast peatlands grew on poorly drained land in the thousands of years following the retreat of continental glaciers.

transpiration   the escape of water from plant leaves in the form of water vapor.

trophic level   each step in a food chain. About 90 percent of the energy available to an organism is lost at each step.

understory   the part of the forest just below the canopy that is made up of the leaves and branches of shorter trees.

zooplankton   drifting, microscopic aquatic animals. Small fish and other small organisms eat these zooplankton.

Further Exploration

Books

Burnie, David. *Eyewitness Books: Tree*. New York: Alfred A. Knopf, 1988.

Hirschi, Ron. *Save Our Forests*. New York: Delacorte Press, 1993.

Hora, Bayard, ed. *Trees and Forests of the World*. 2 vols. New York: Marshall Cavendish, 1990.

Lampton, Christopher. *Forest Fire: A Disaster Book*. New York: Houghton Mifflin, 1992.

Mania, Cathy, and Robert Mania. *A Forest's Life: From Meadow to Mature Woodland*. Danbury, CT: Watts, 1997.

Olson, Sigurd F. *The Singing Wilderness, Listening Point, The Lonely Land*. Reprinted as the Fesler-Lampert Minnesota Heritage Book Series. Minneapolis: University of Minnesota Press, 1997.

Pipes, Rose. *Forests and Woodlands*. Chatham, NJ: Raintree Steck-Vaughn, 1999.

Sadler, Tony. *Forests and Their Environment*. New York: Oxford University Press, 1994.

Scott, Michael. *The Young Oxford Book of Ecology*. New York: Oxford University Press, 1995.

Stensaas, Mark. *Canoe Country Flora: Plants and Trees of the North Woods and Boundary Waters*. Duluth, MN: Pfeifer-Hamilton, 1996.

Organizations

Minnesota Department of Natural Resources
Information Center
500 Lafayette Road
St. Paul, MN 55155
(651) 296-6157 or
toll-free in state: (888) 646-6367
www.dnr.state.mn.us

Superior National Forest
8901 Grand Avenue Place
Duluth, MN 55808
(218) 626-4300 TTY: (218) 626-4399

Friends of Pukaskwa National Park
General Delivery, Heron Bay
Ontario P0T 1R0
(807) 229-0801, extension 233

Voyageurs National Park
Lake States Interpretive Association
3131 Highway 53
International Falls, MN 56649
(218) 283-2103

Index

Page numbers for illustrations are in **boldface**.